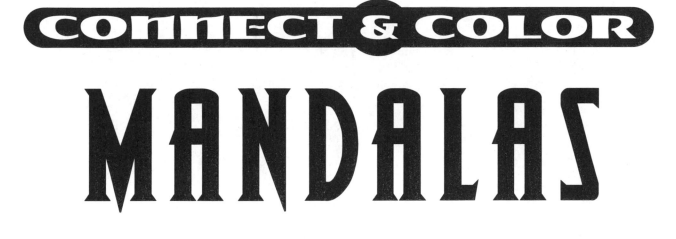

CONNECT & COLOR

MANDALAS

Racehorse Publishing books may be purchased in bulk at special discounts for sales promotion, corporate gifts, fund-raising, or educational purposes. Special editions can also be created to specifications. For details, contact the Special Sales Department, Skyhorse Publishing, 307 West 36th Street, 11th Floor, New York, NY 10018 or info@skyhorsepublishing.com.

Racehorse Publishing™ is a pending trademark of Skyhorse Publishing, Inc.®, a Delaware corporation.

Visit our website at www.skyhorsepublishing.com.

10 9 8 7 6 5 4 3 2 1

Spot illustrations by Mary and Javier Agredo
Mandala art by Sayaka Oeno and Alexander T. Lee
Produced by Hourglass Press llc.

Print ISBN: 978-1-944686-77-2

Printed in the United States of America

CONNECT & COLOR

MANDALAS

An Intricate Coloring and Dot-to-Dot Book

Racehorse Publishing

Dot-to-Dot Guide

○ = Starting Dot

◆ = Last Dot

◑ = Starting/End Dot

⬤ = Overlapping

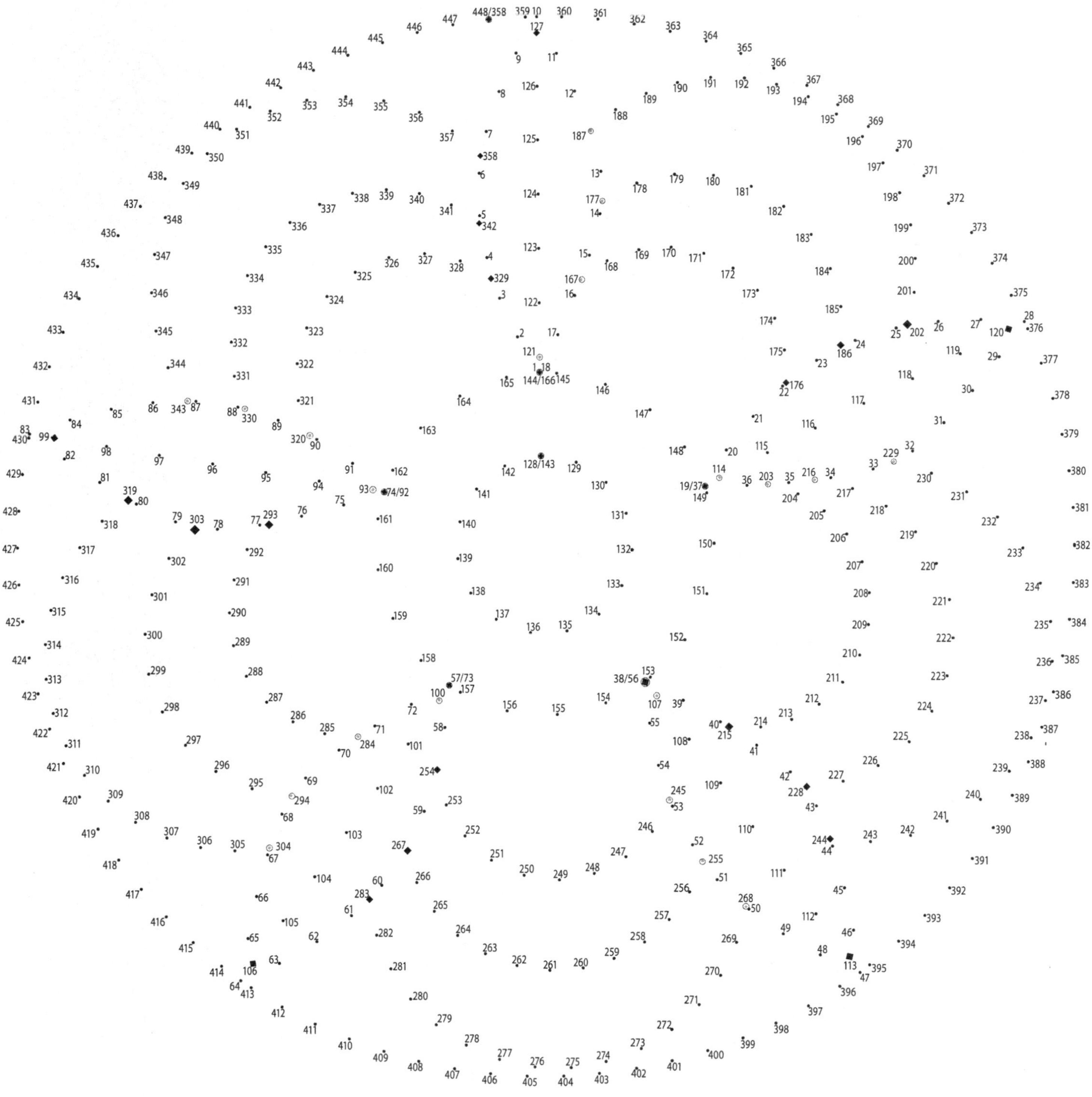

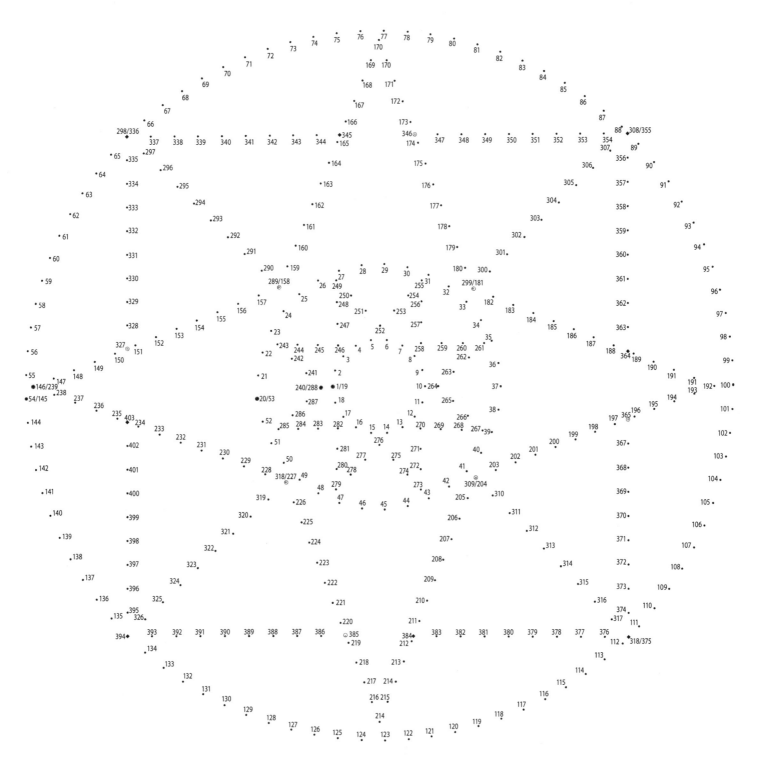

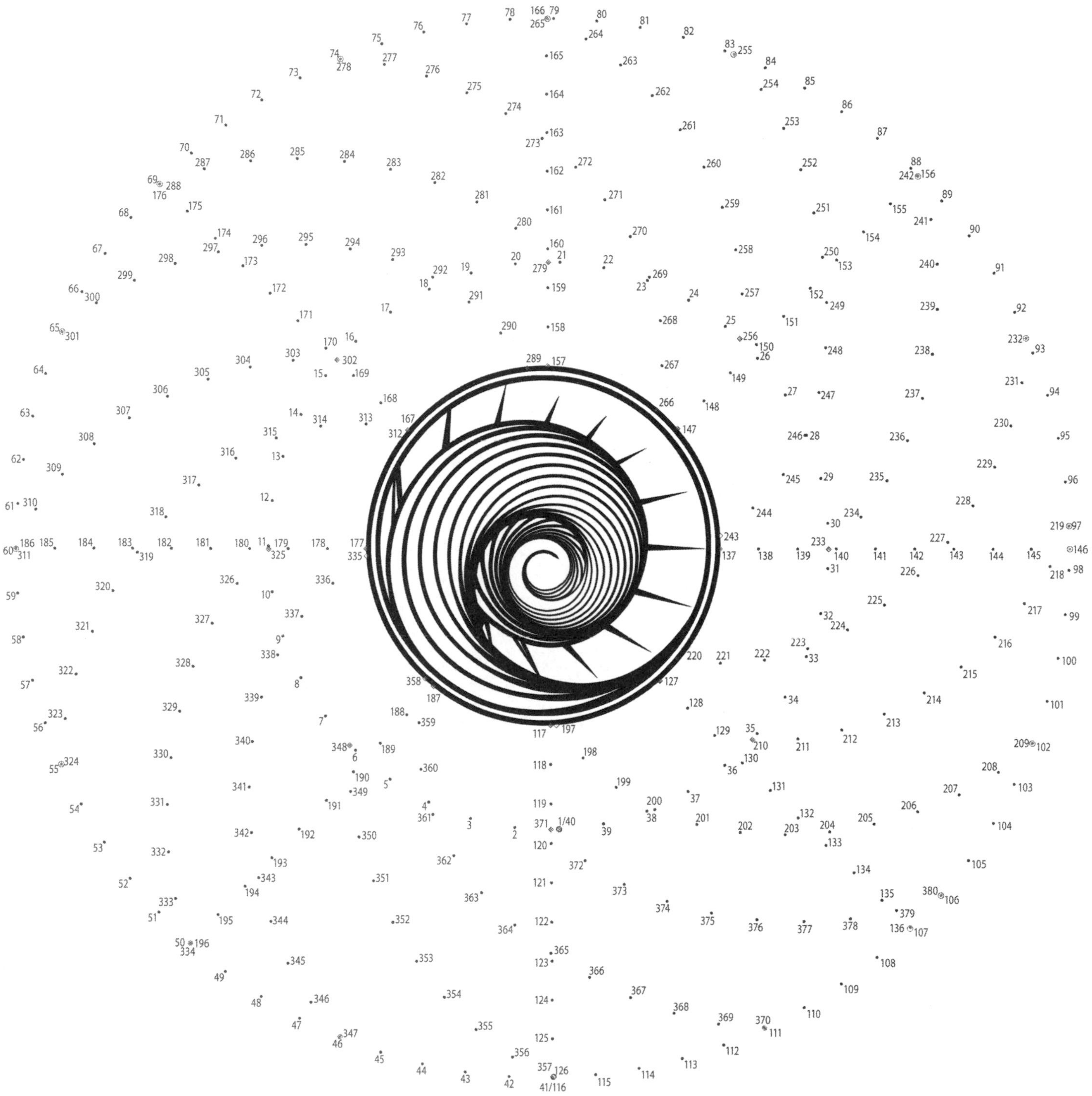

254 362 433 434 435 436 437 438 439 440 441 442 264 443 444 445 446 447 448 449 450 451 452 453 454 455 456 457 458 459

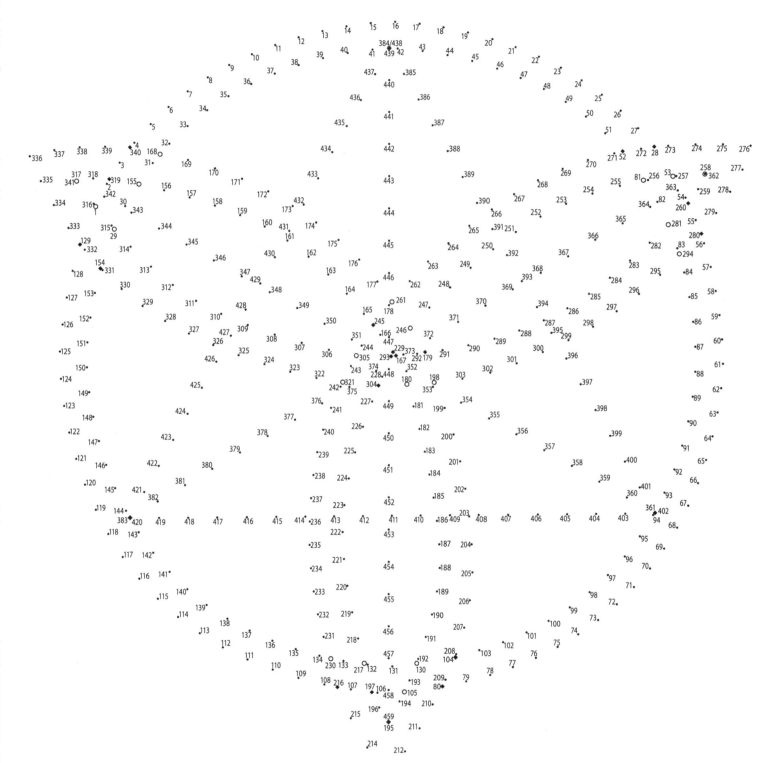

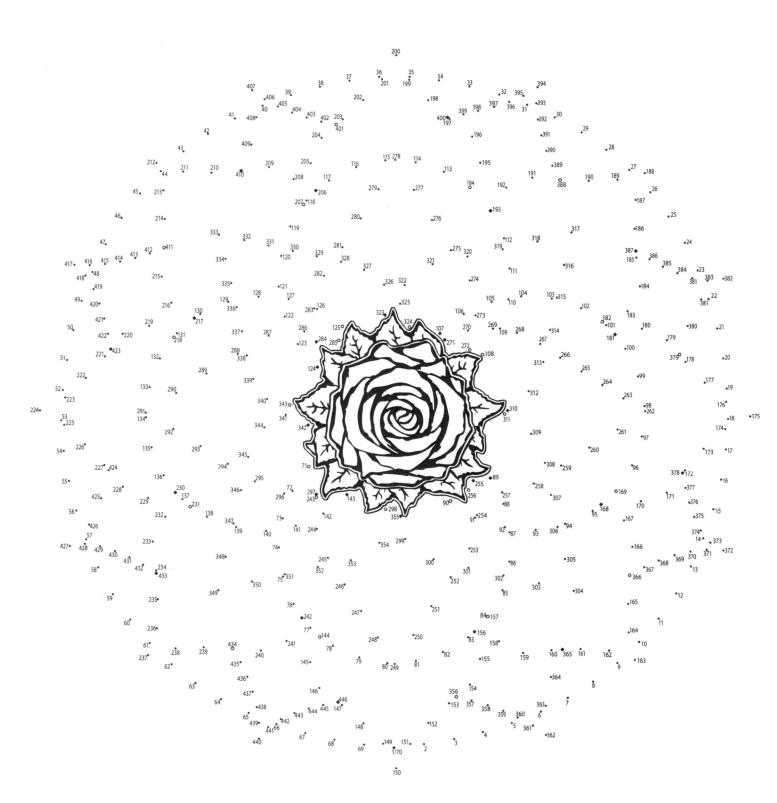

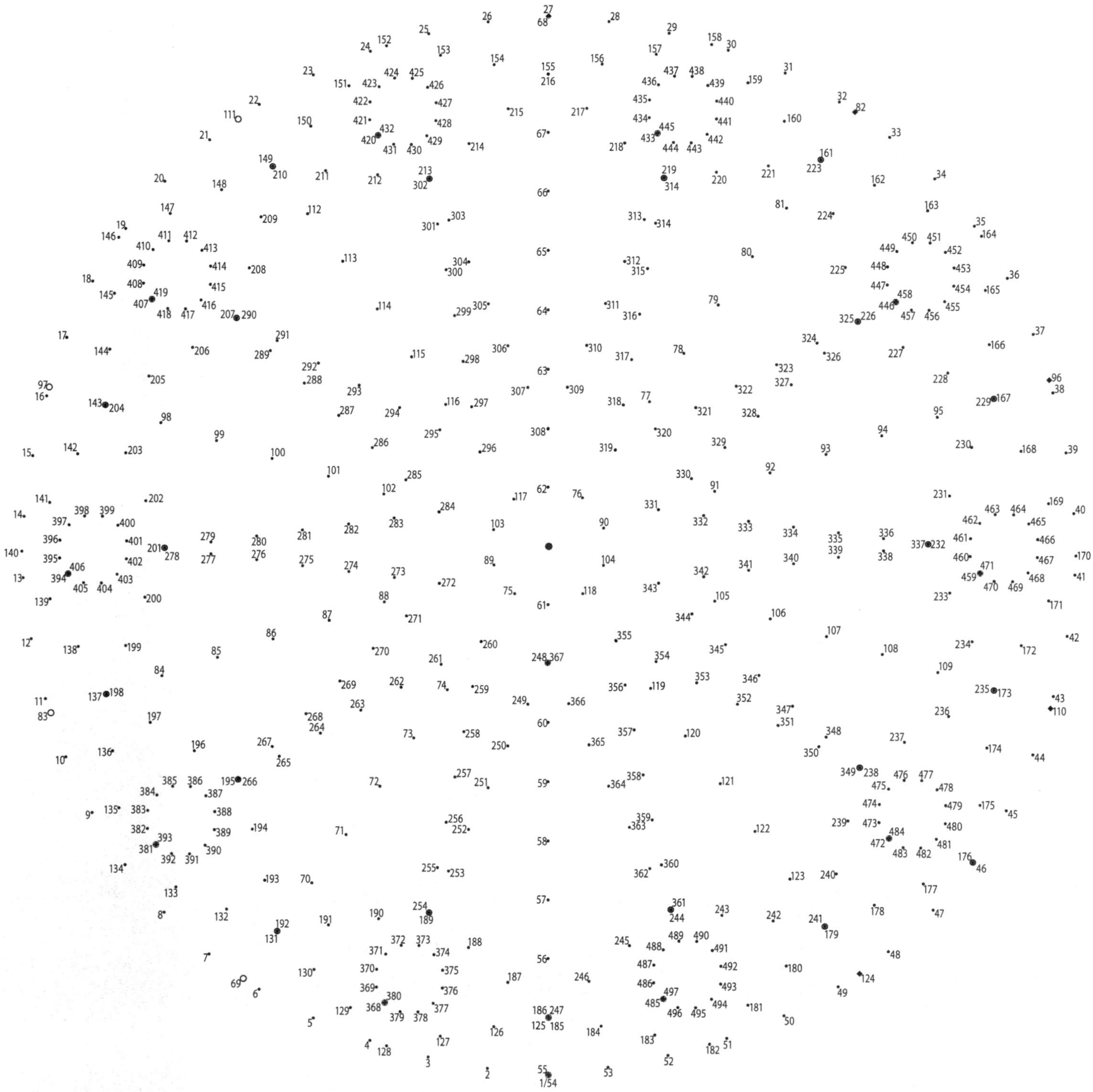

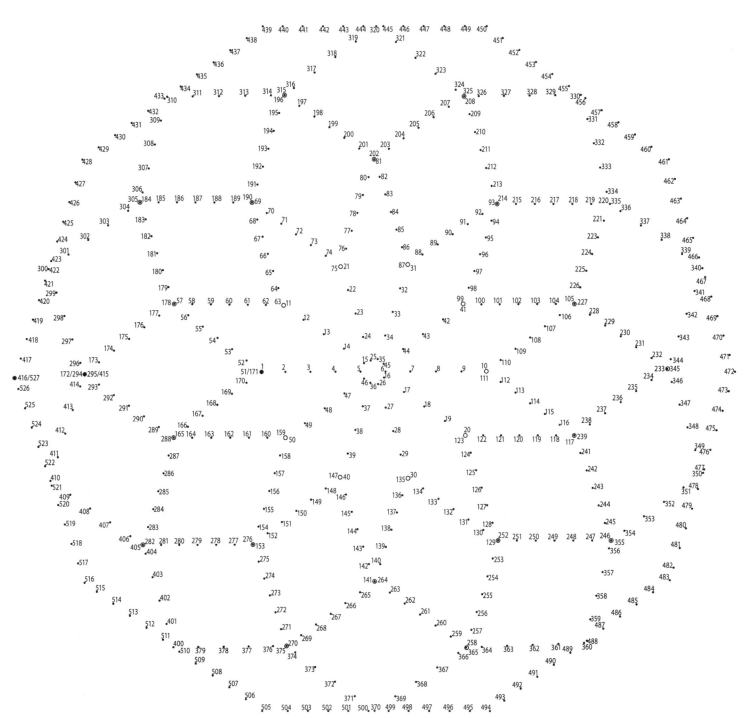

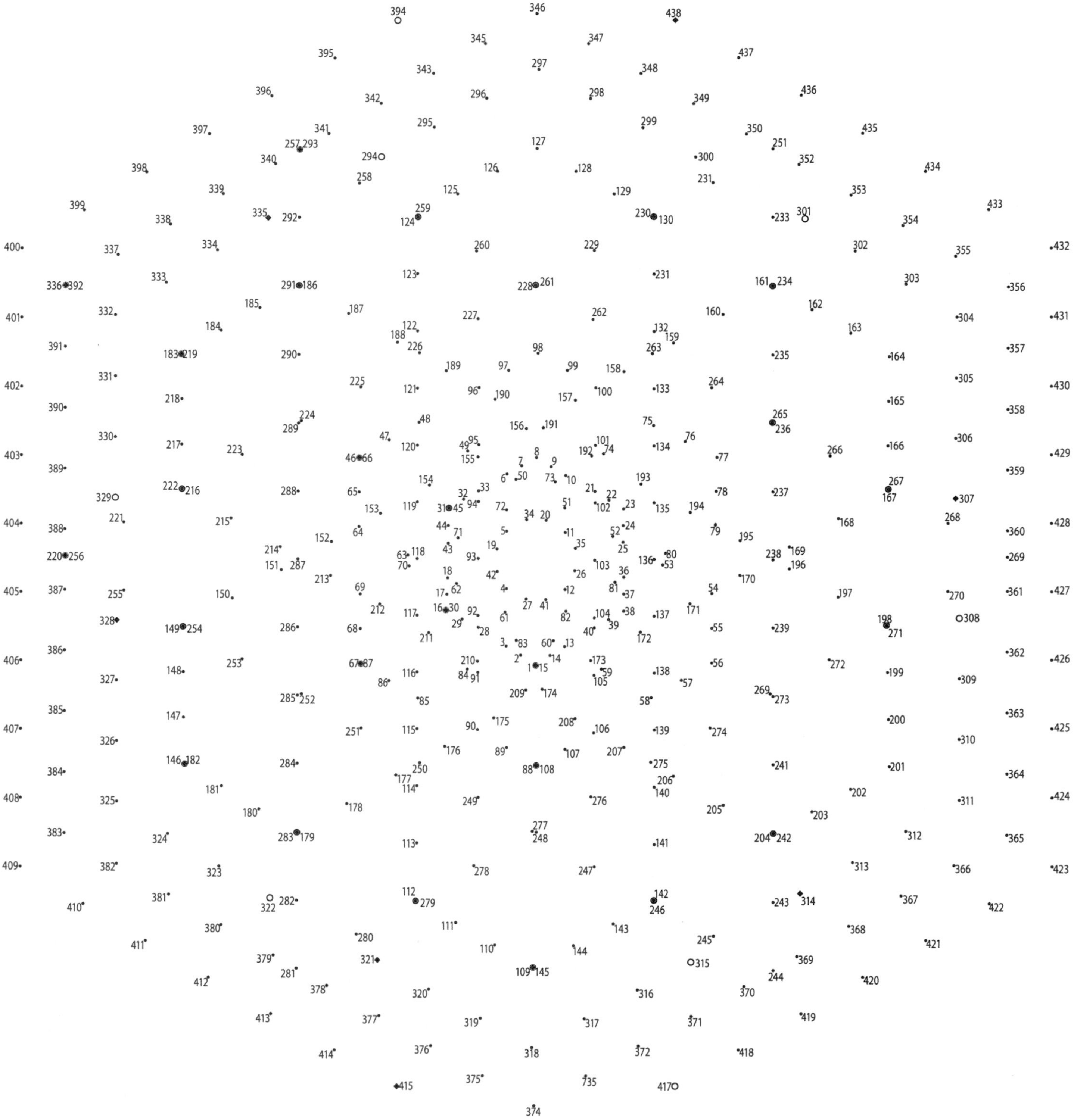

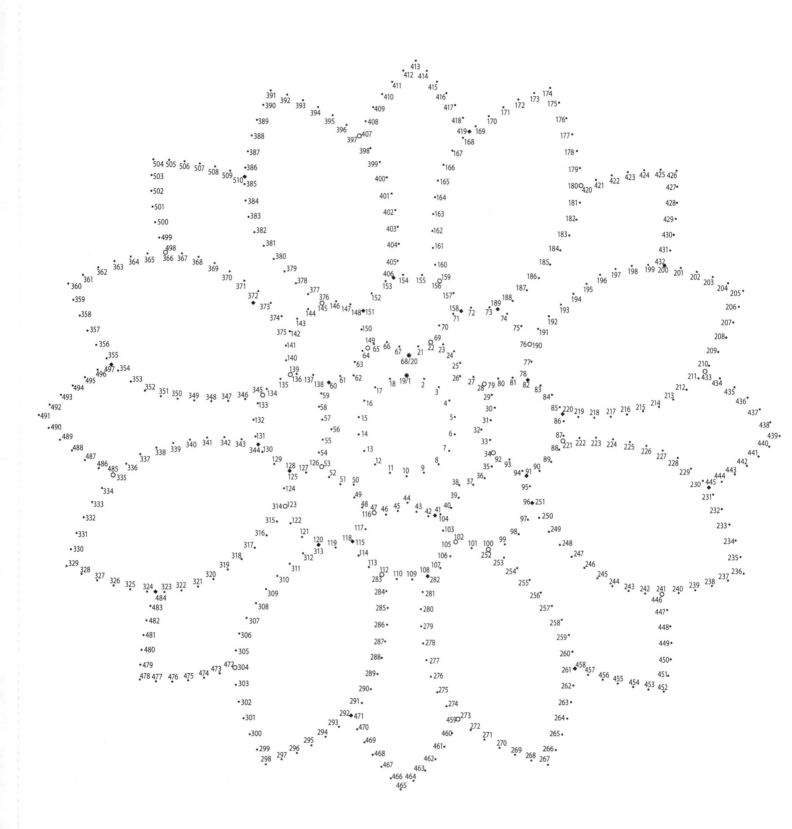

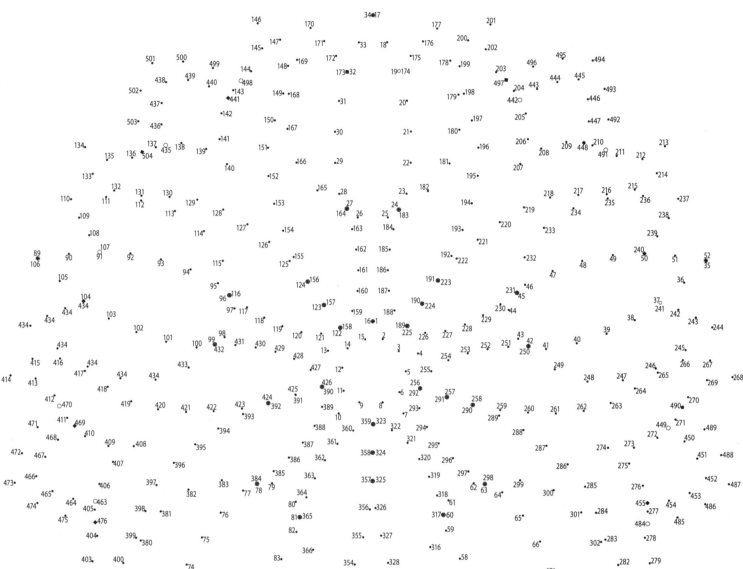

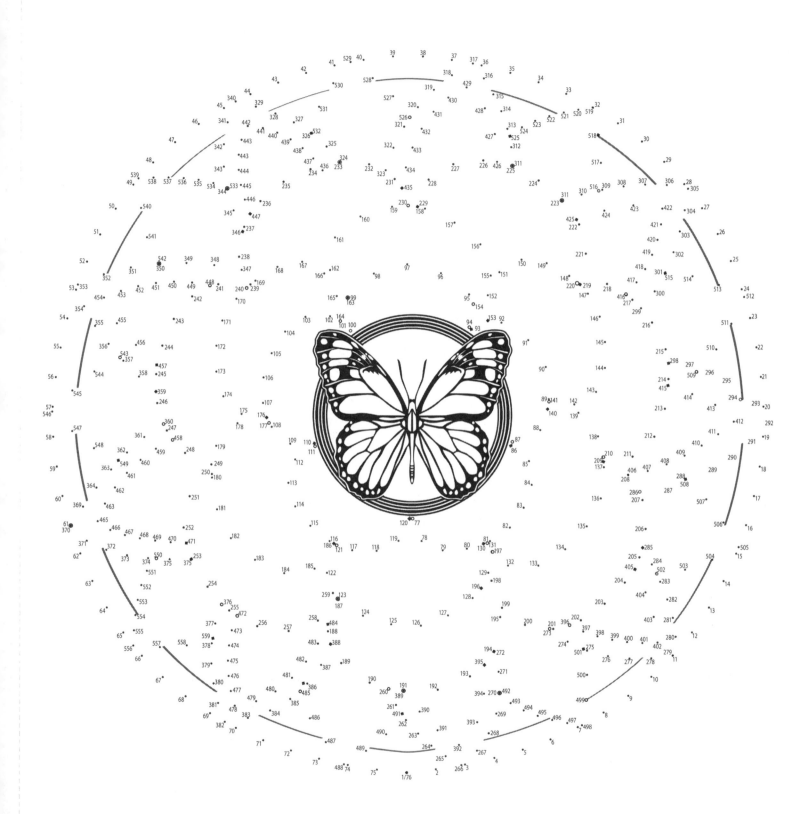

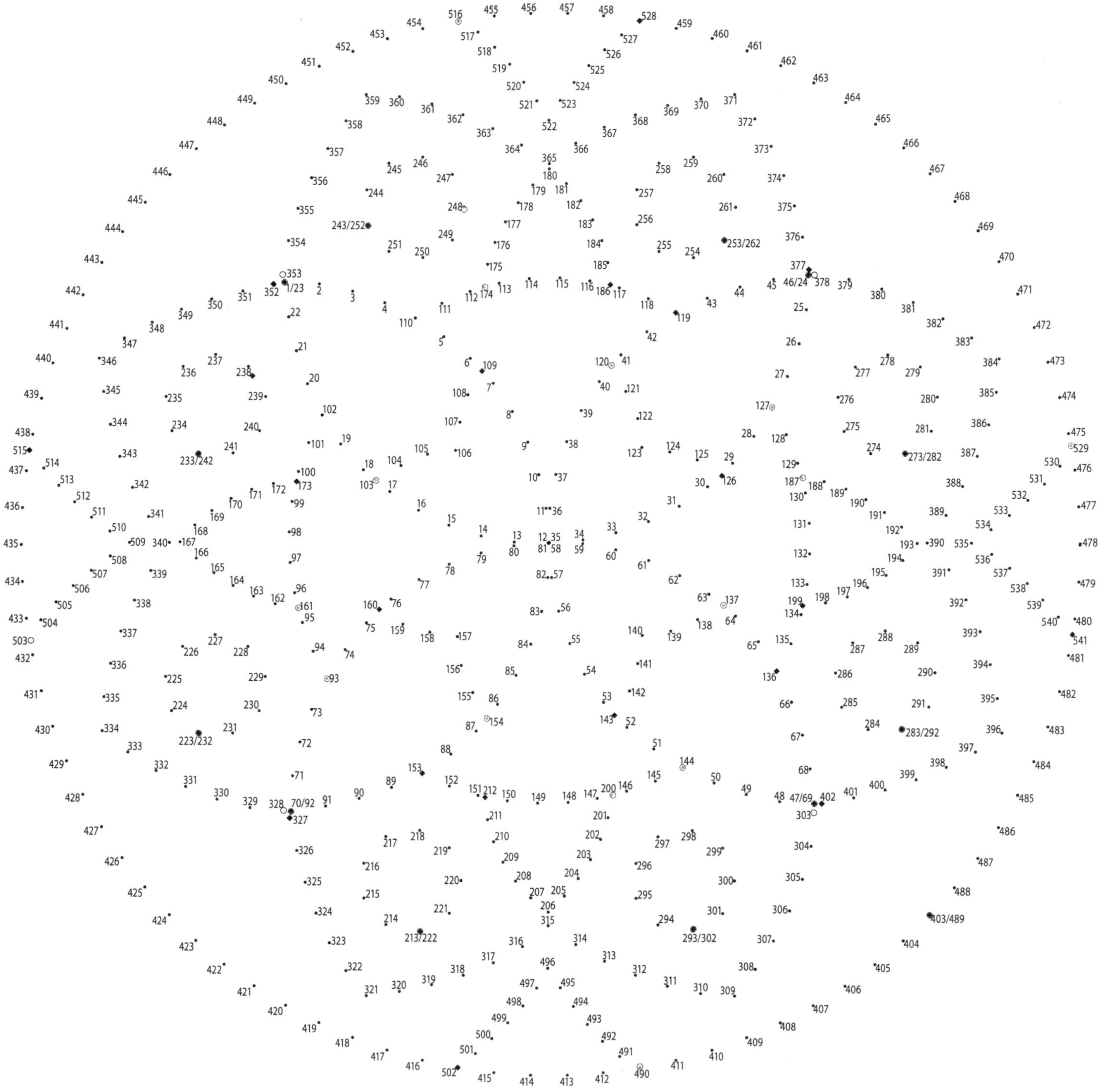

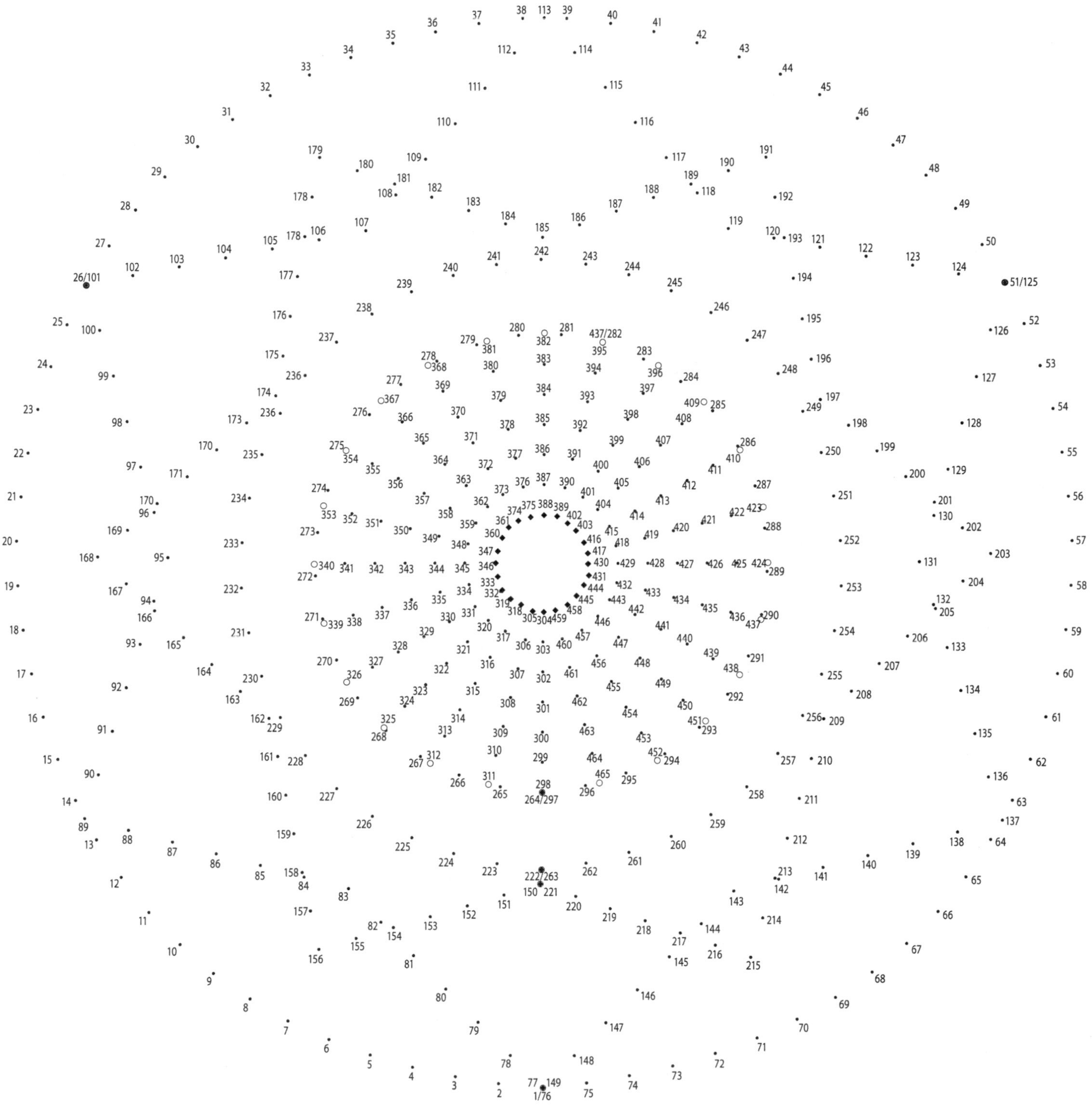

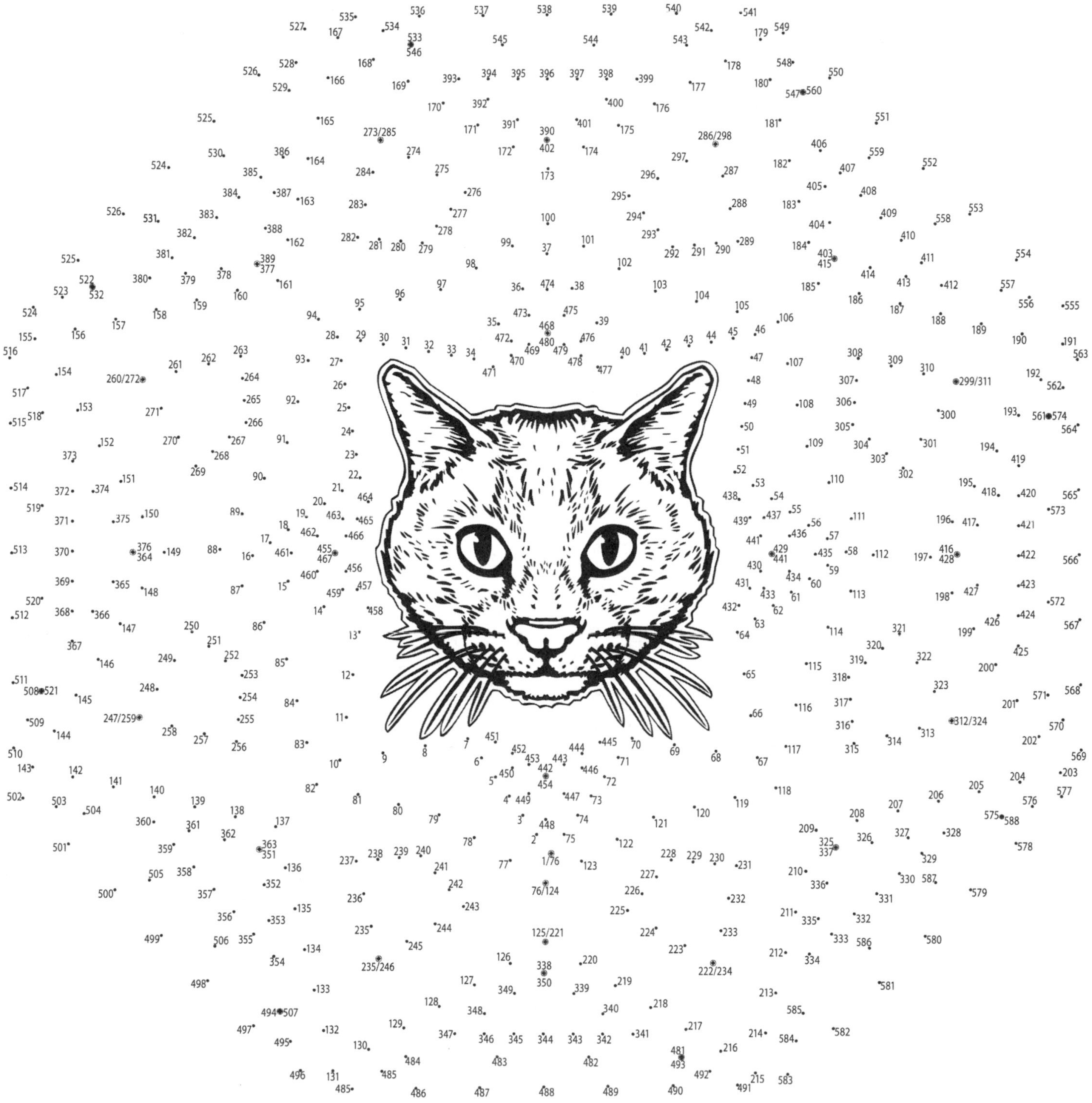

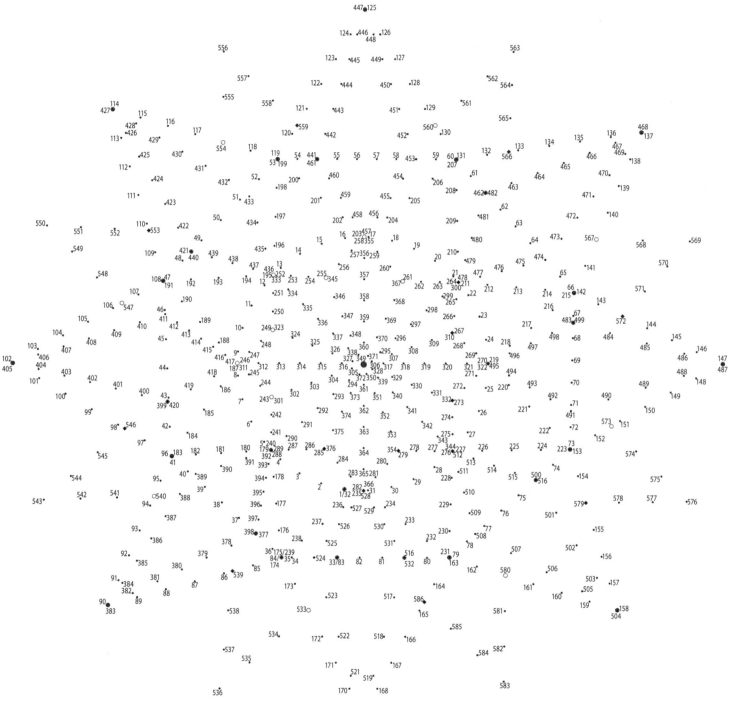

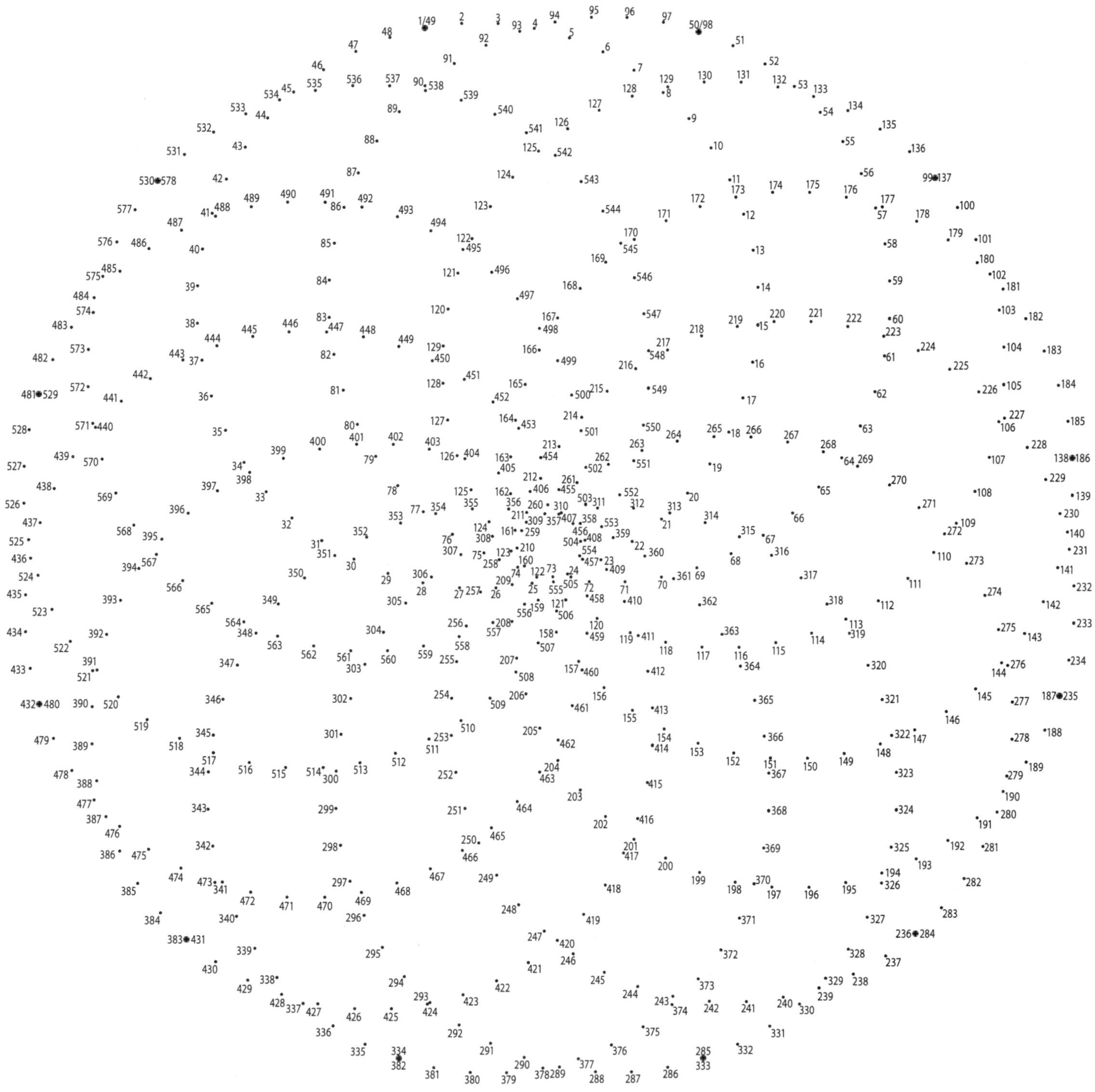

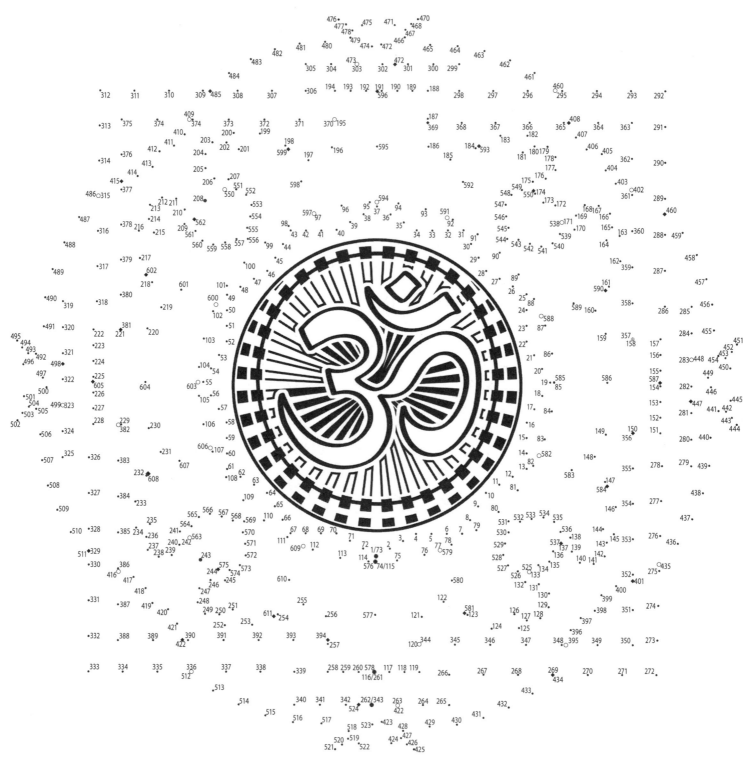

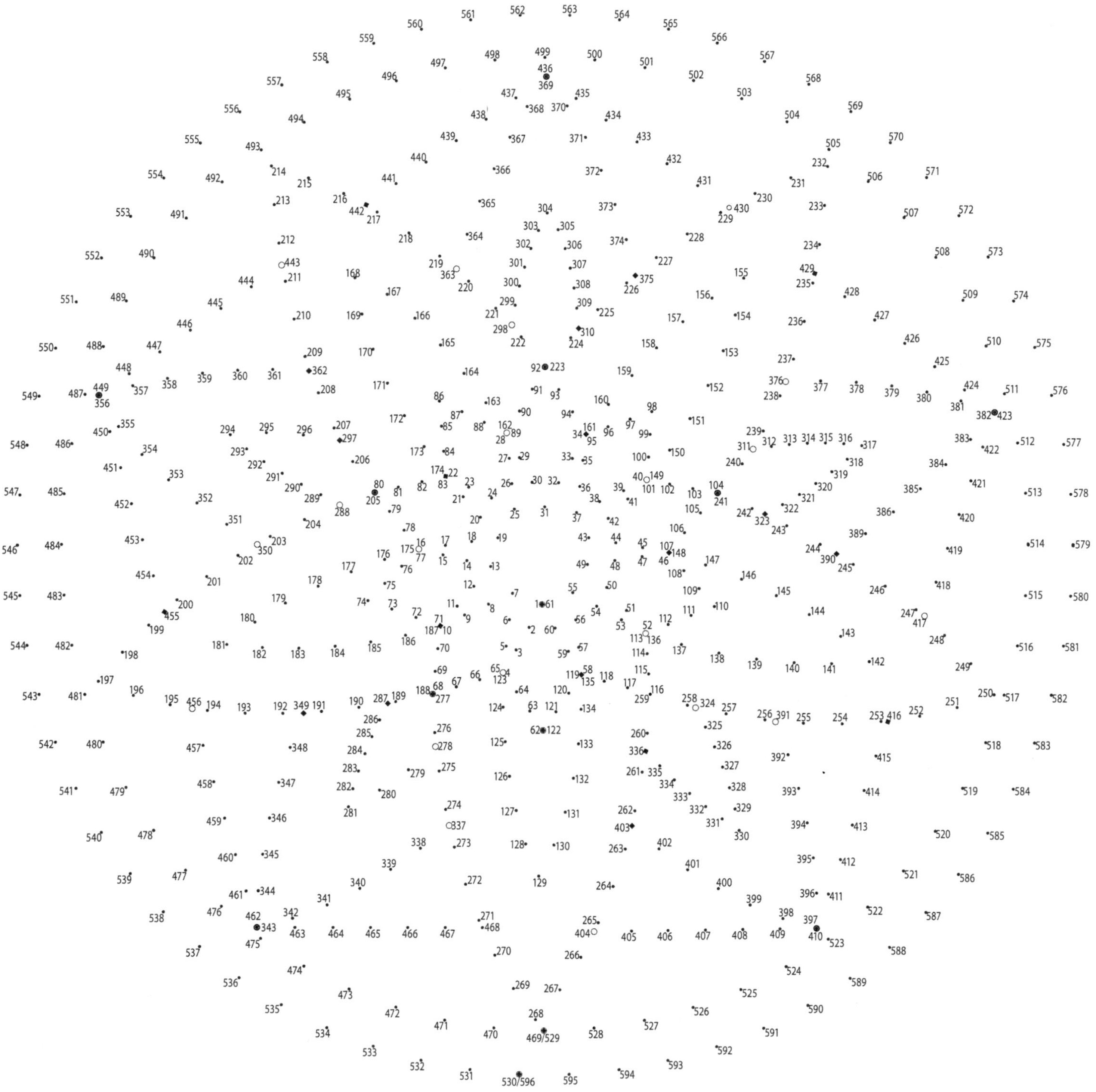

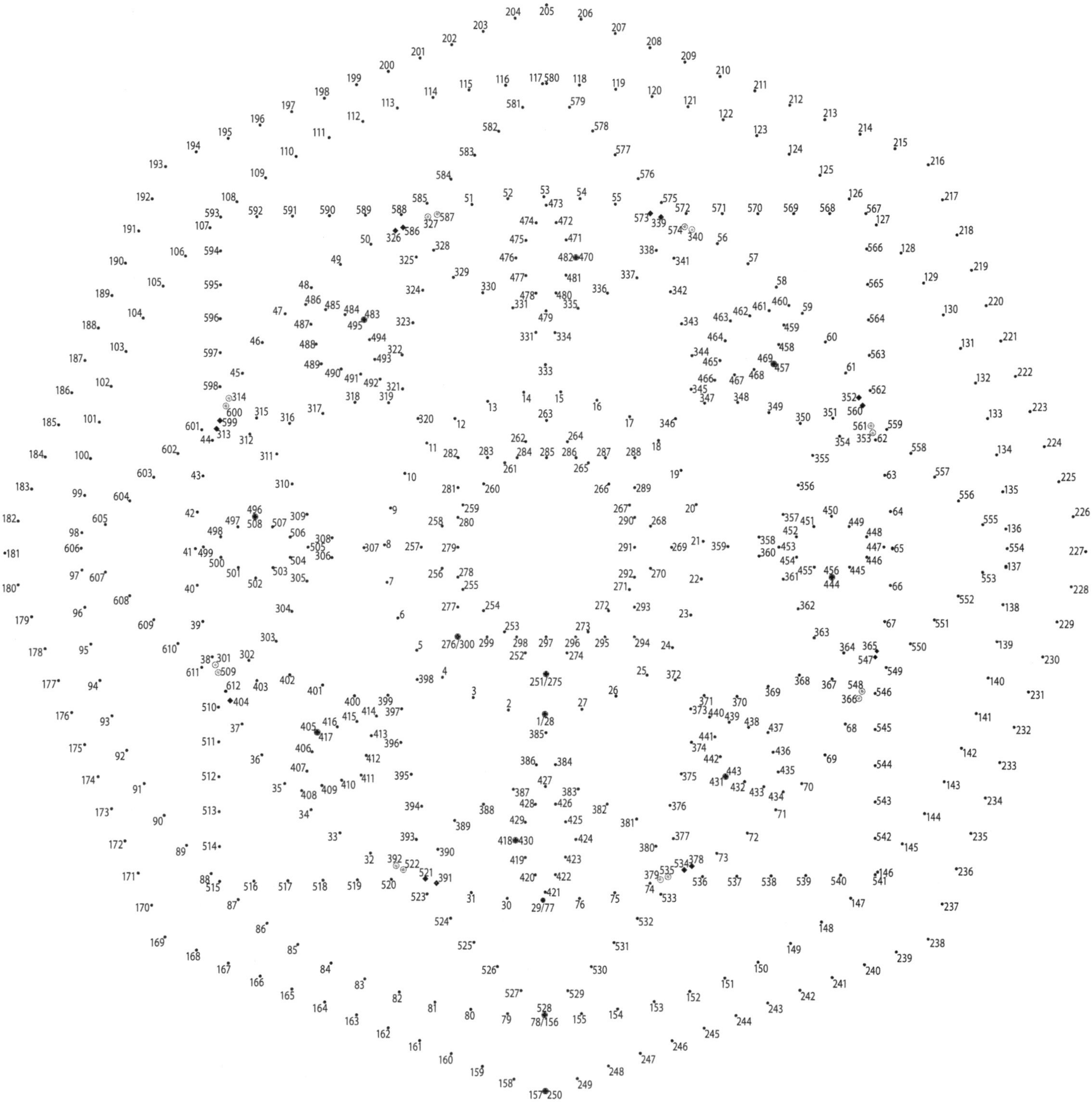

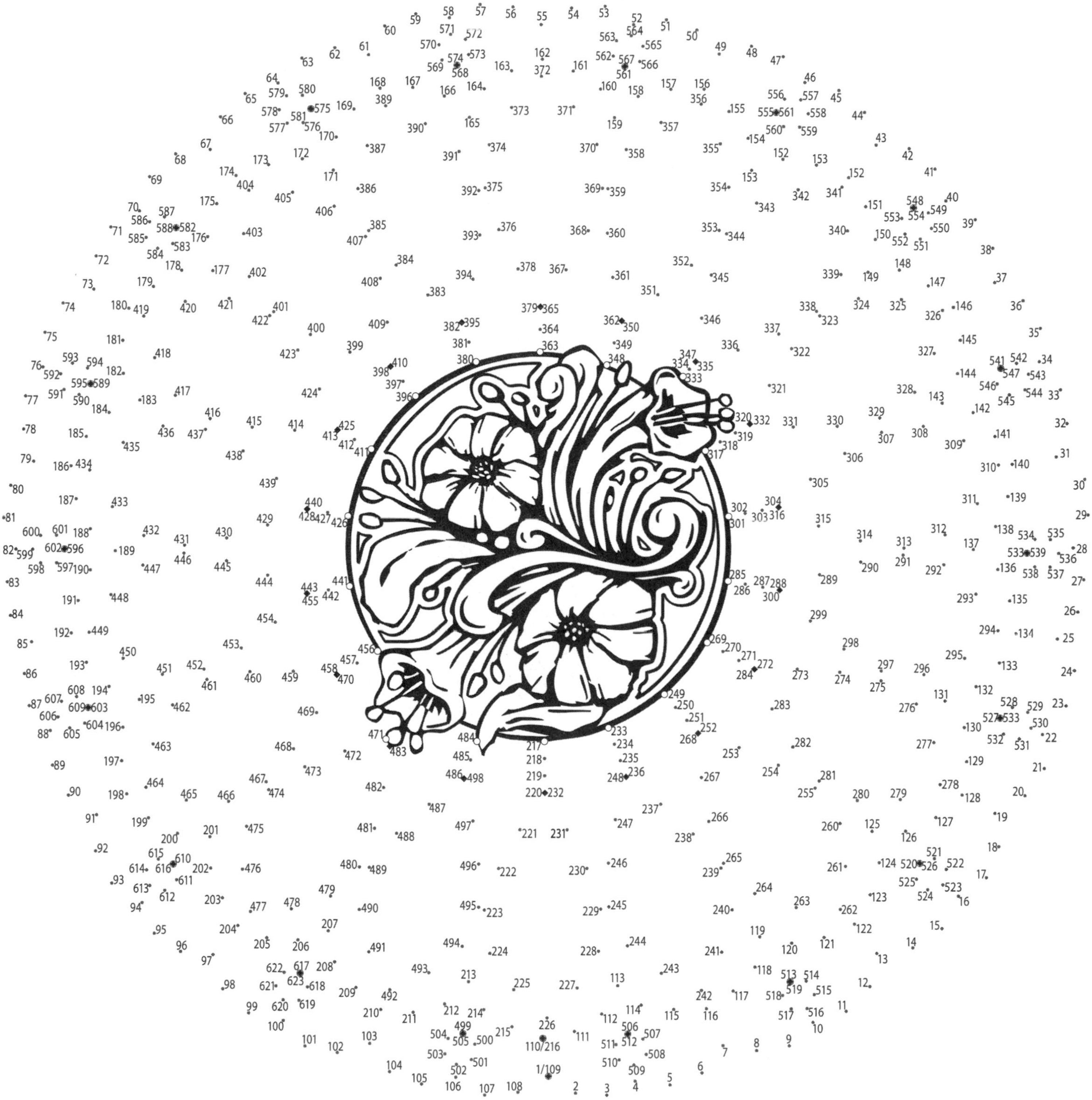

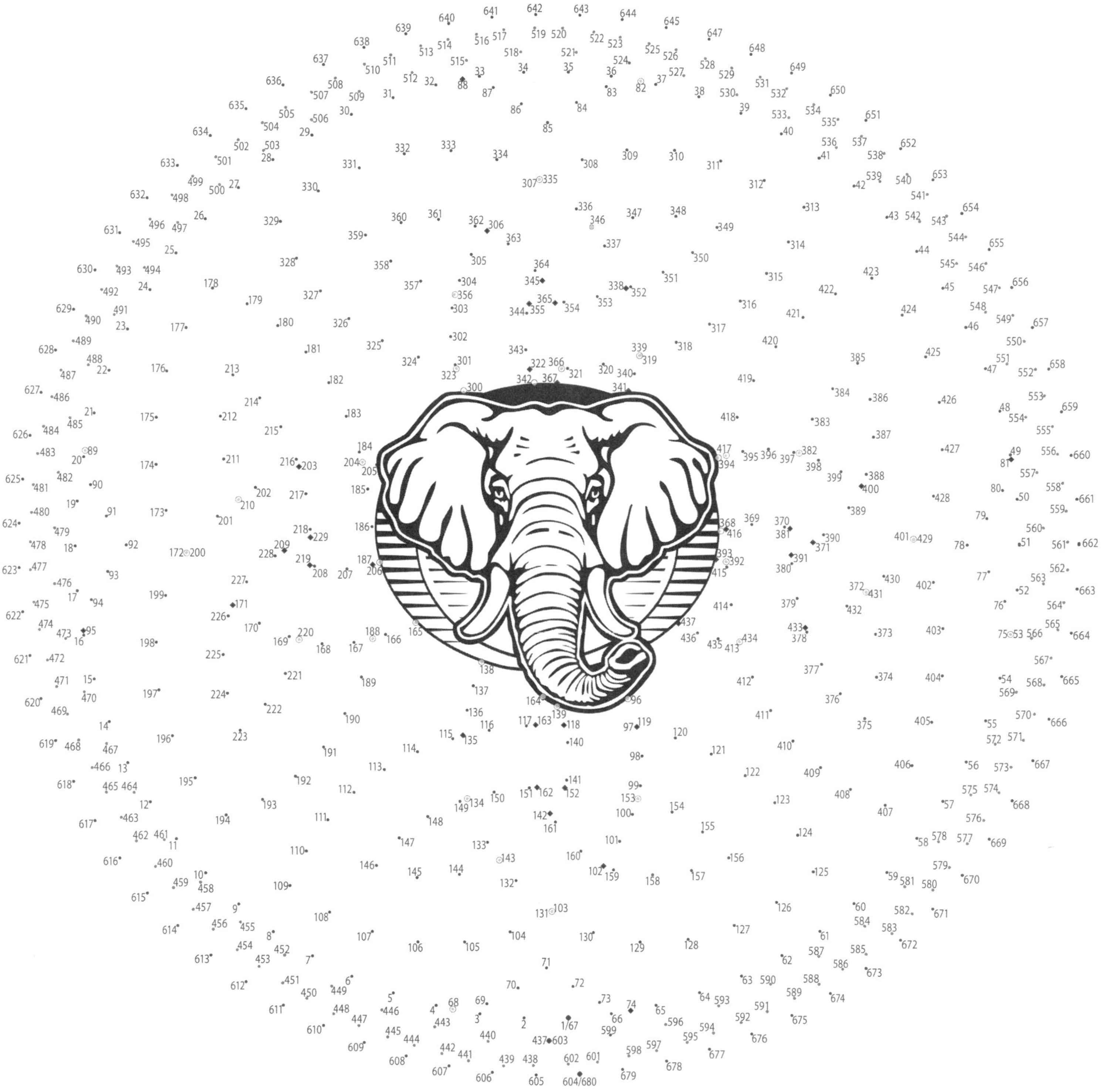

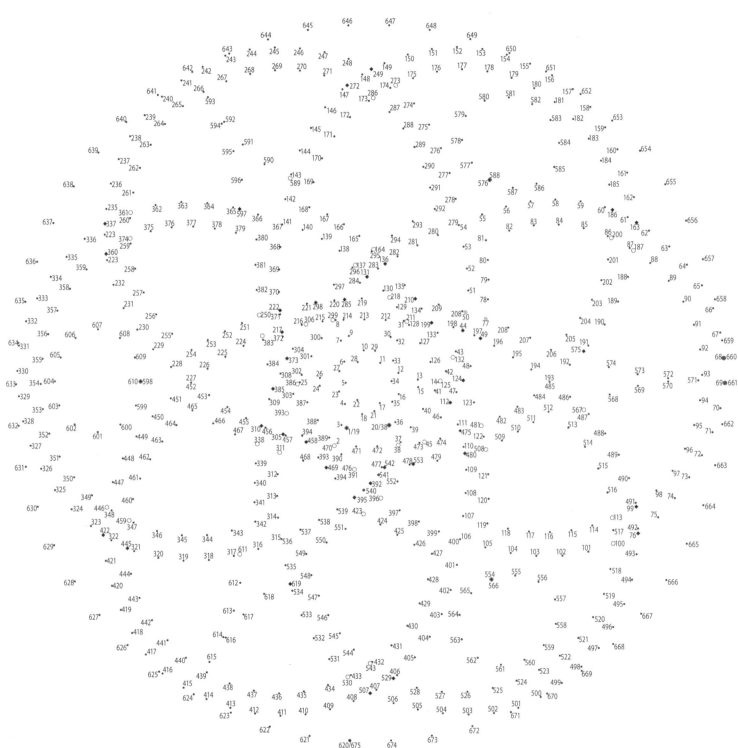

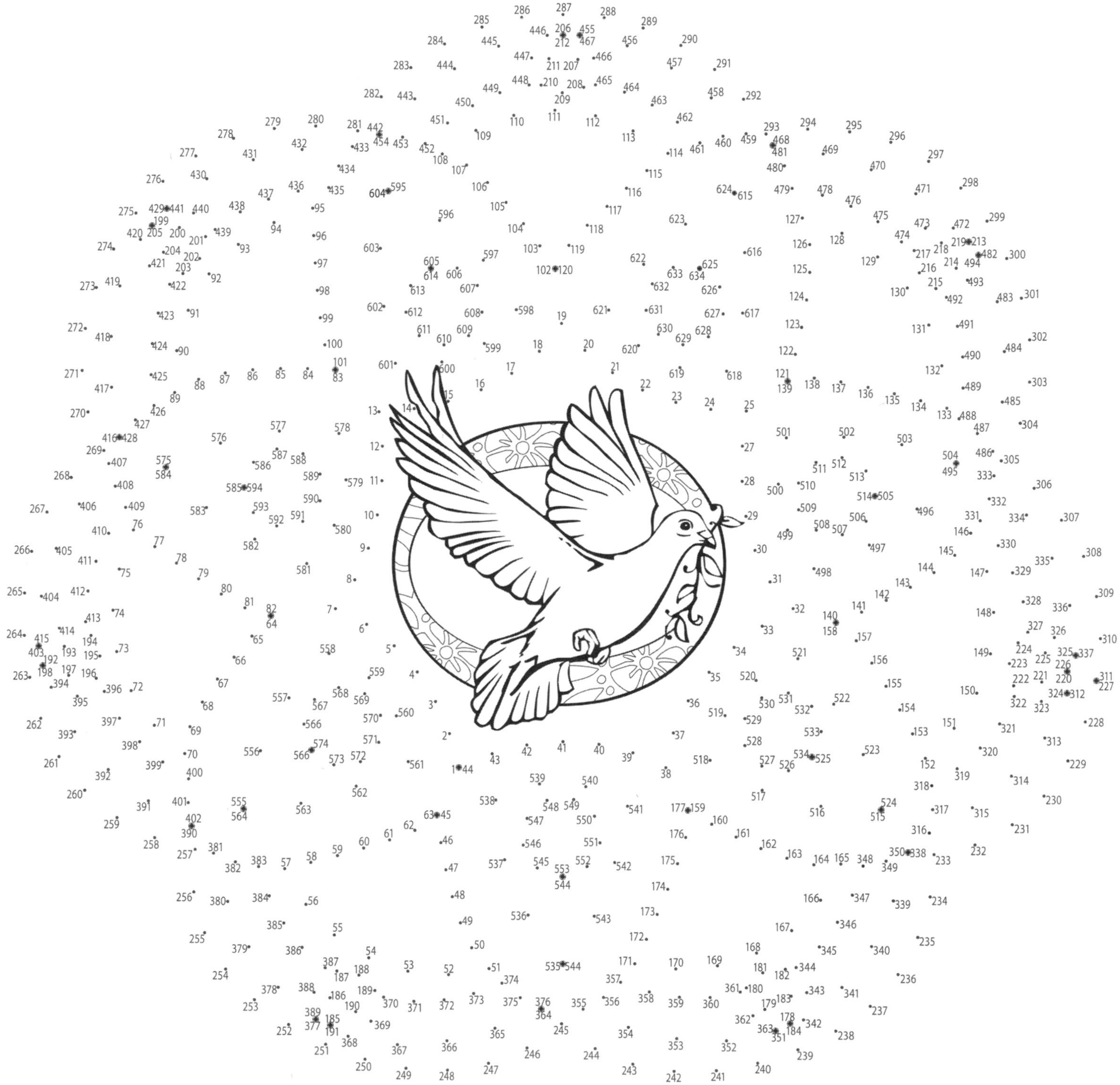

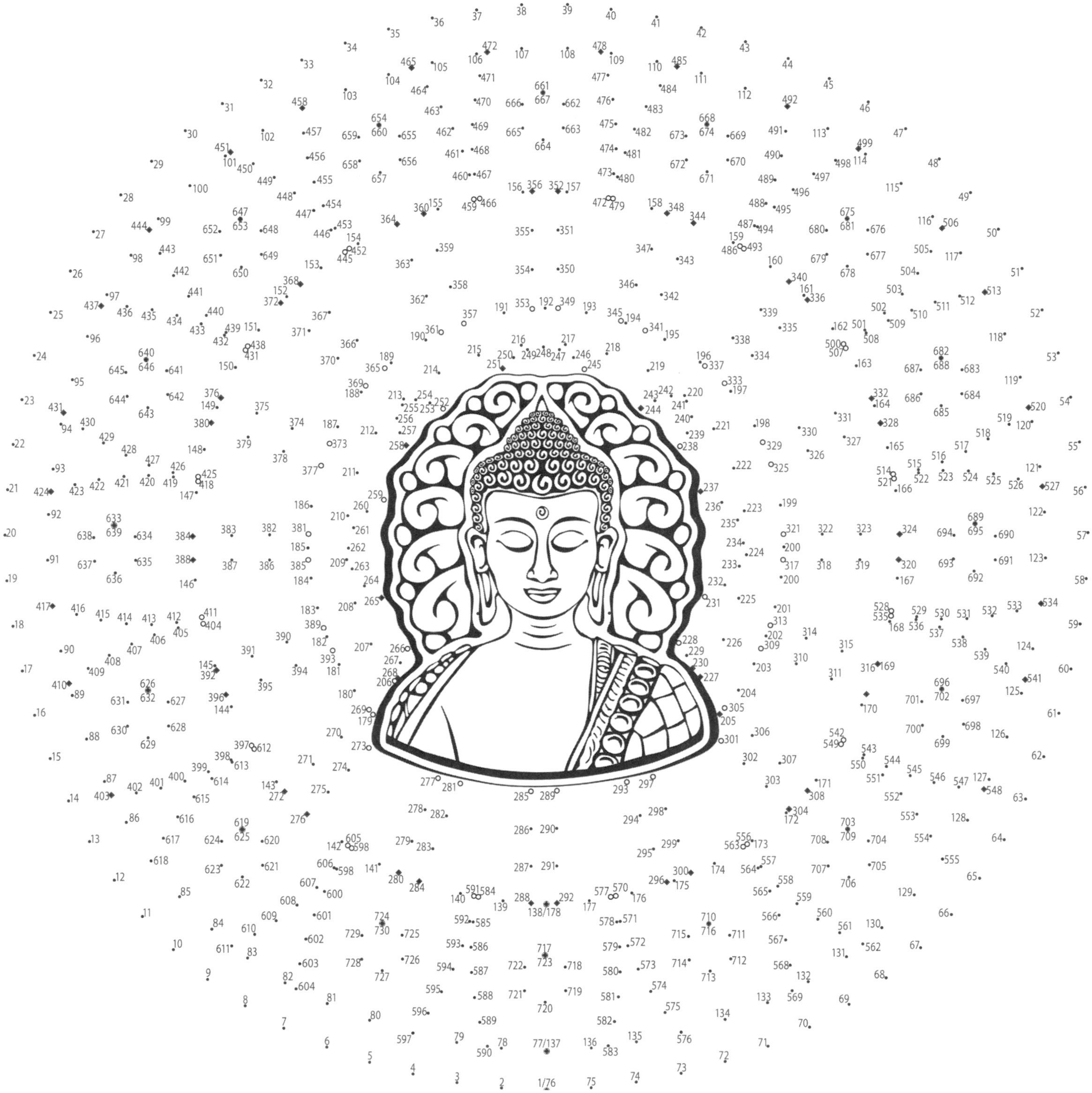

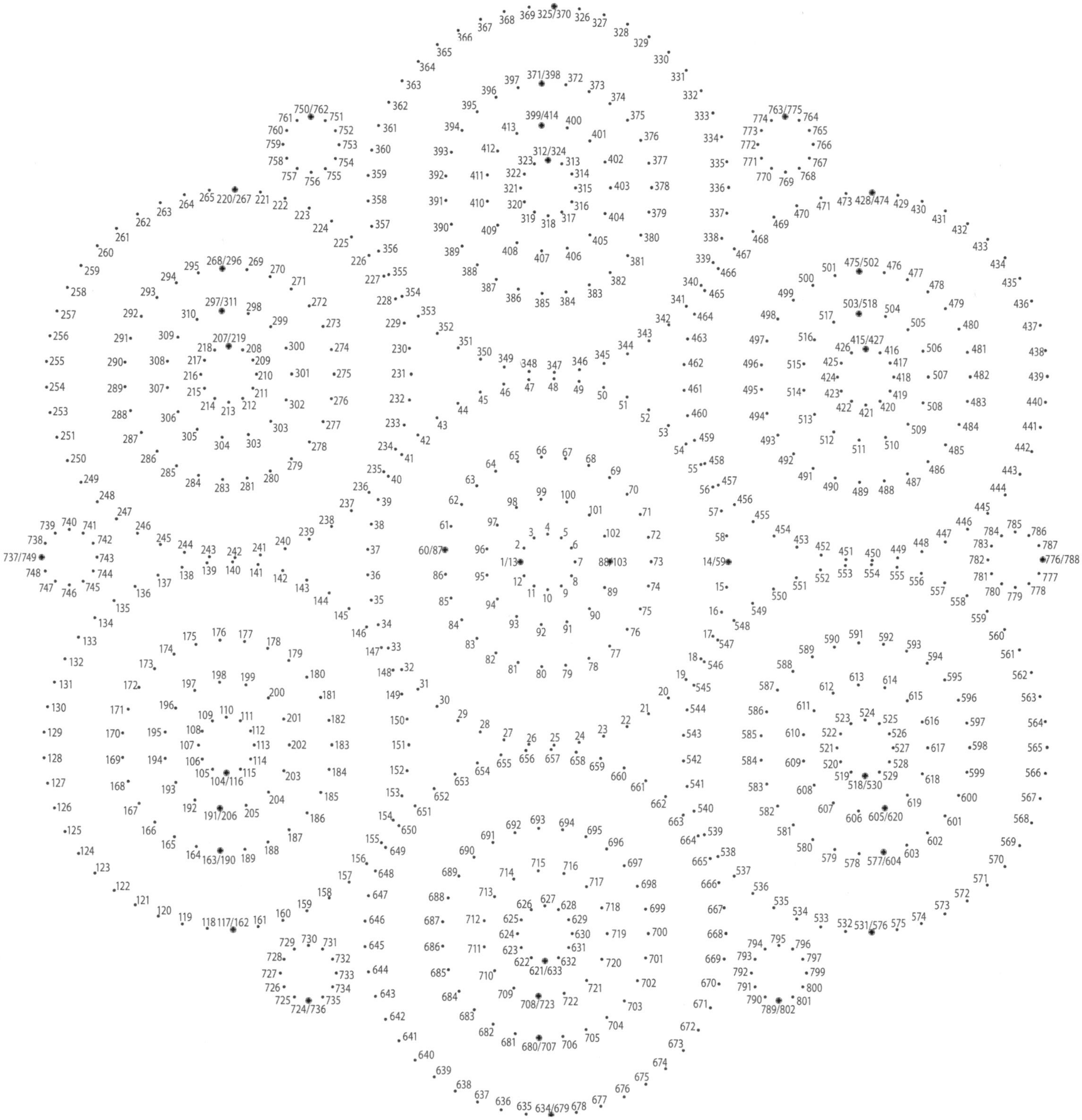

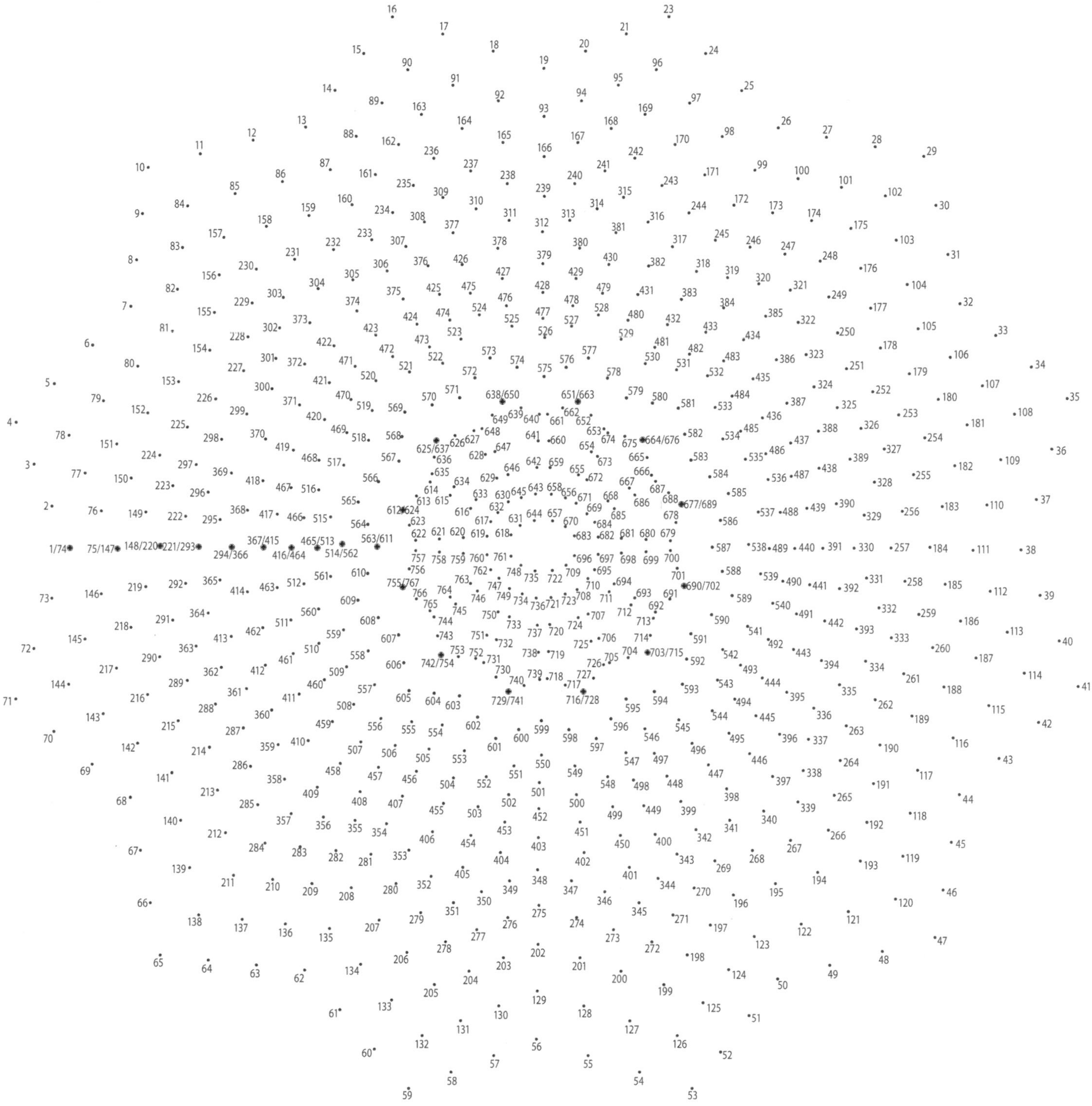

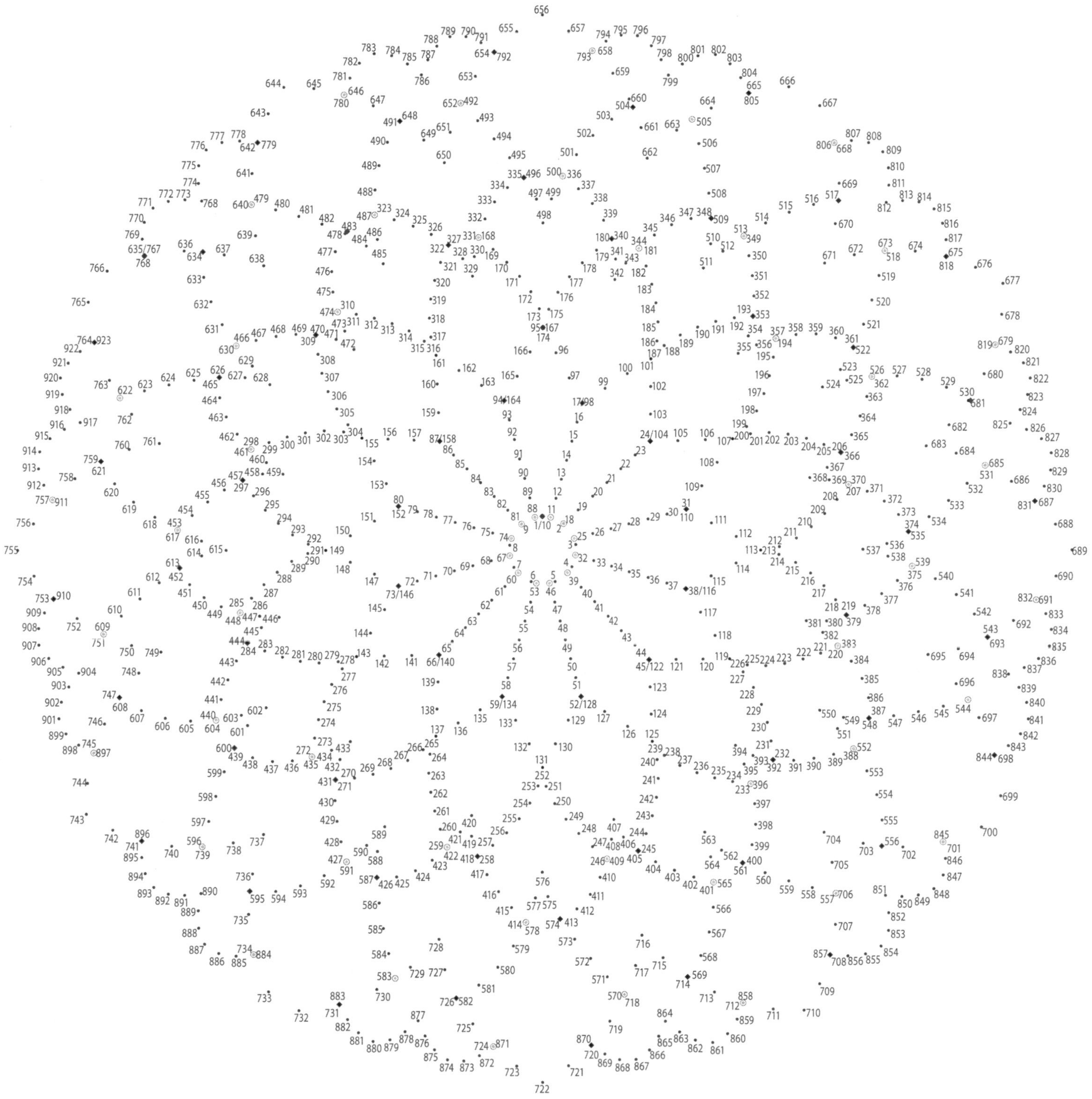

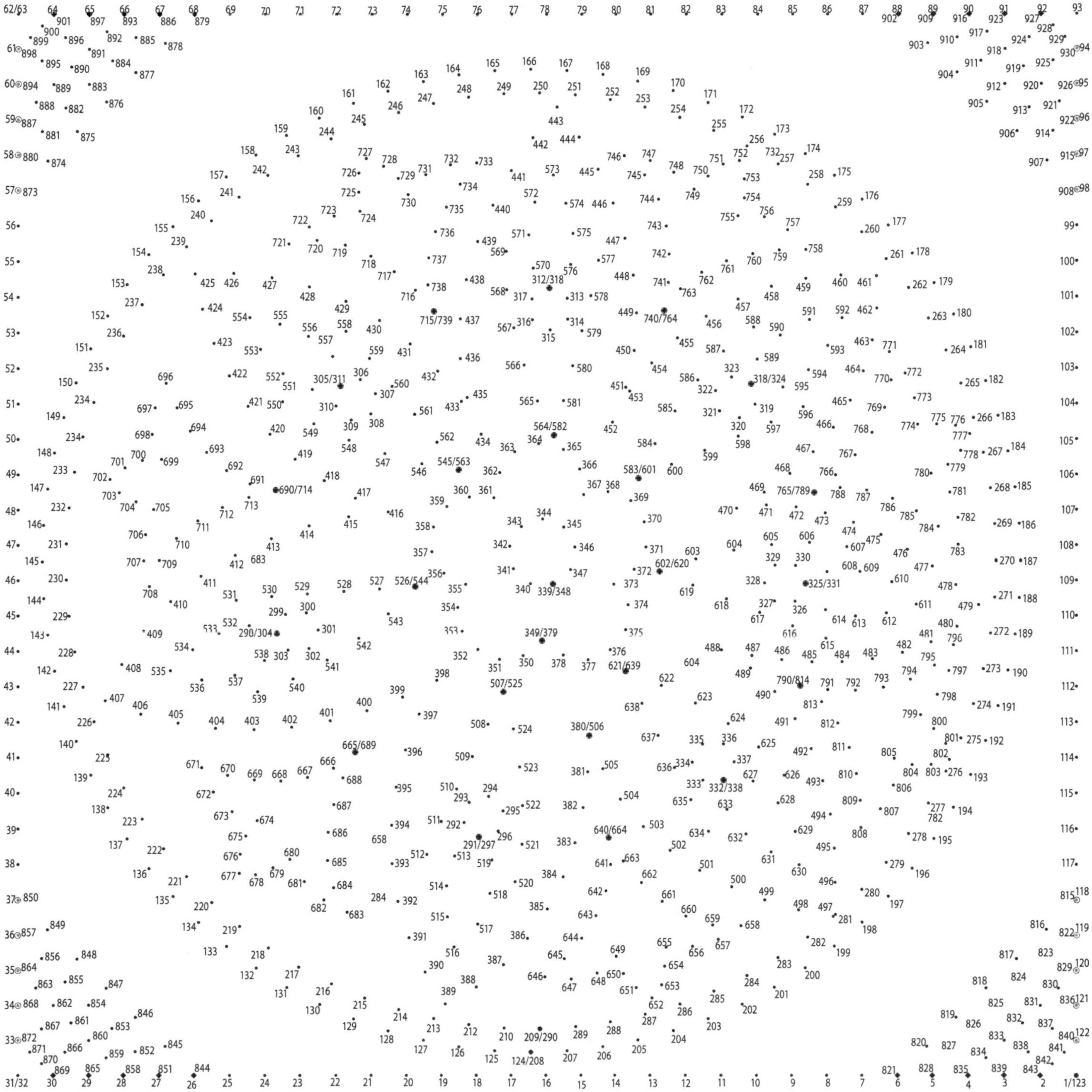

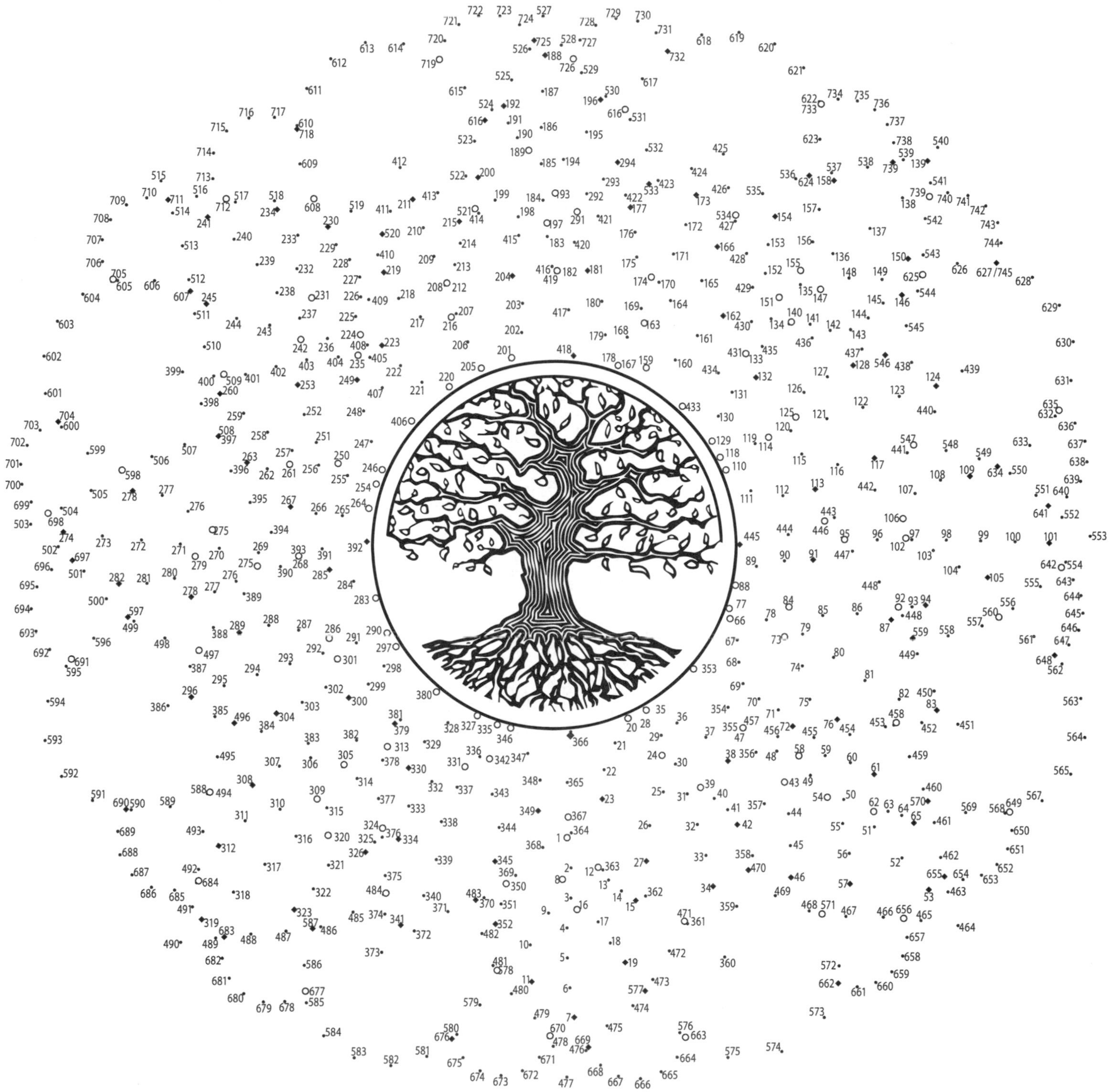

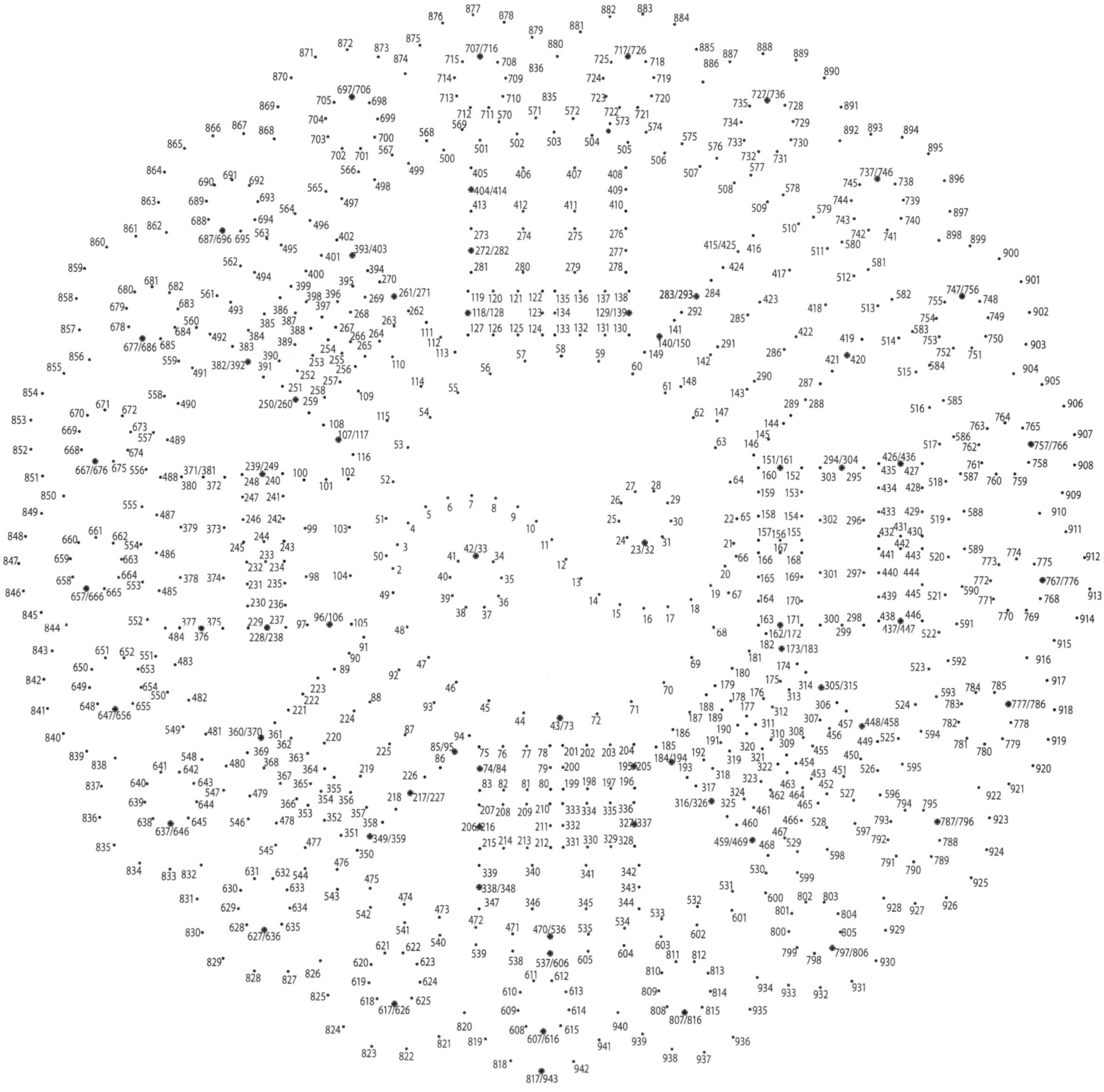

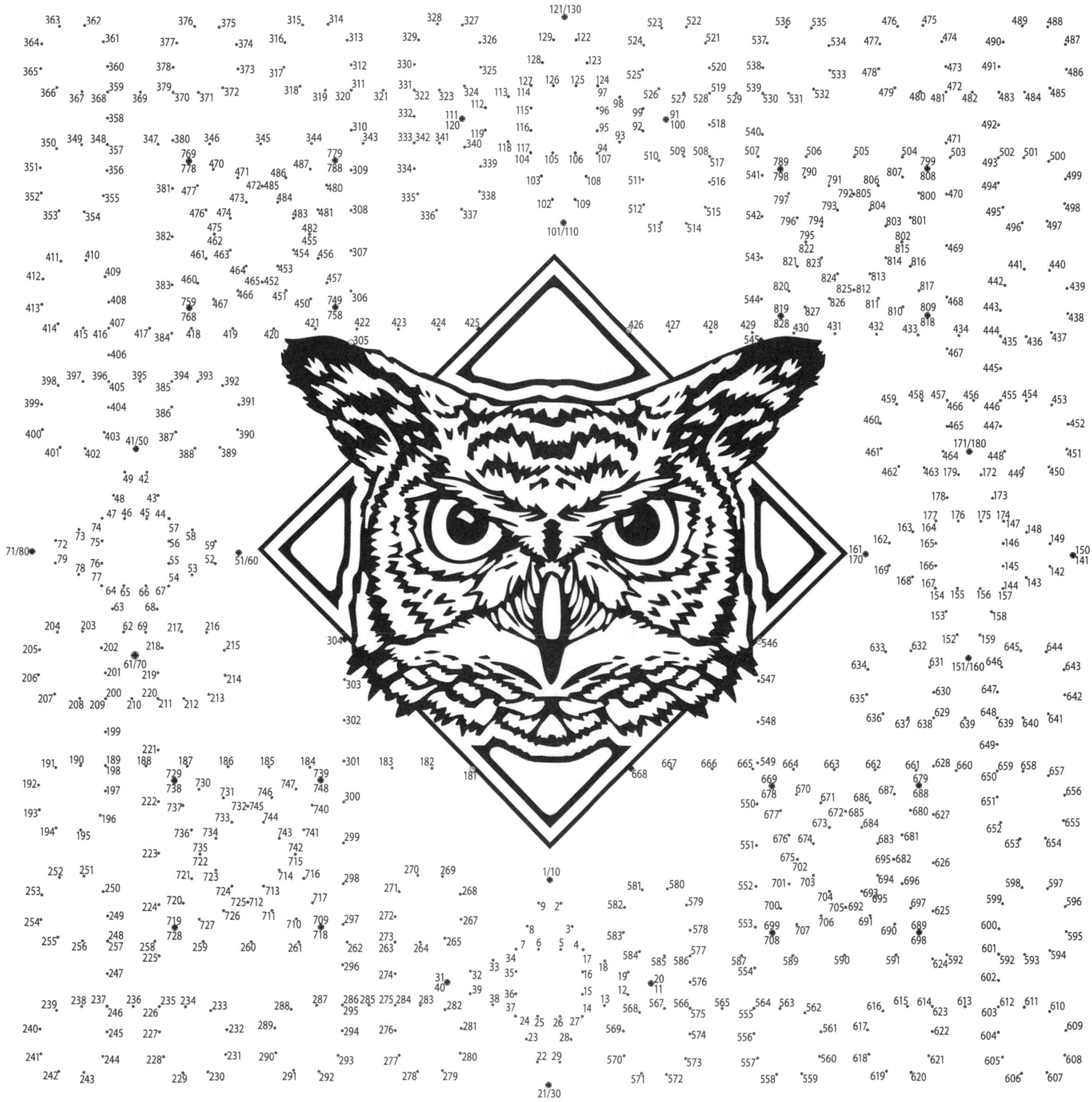

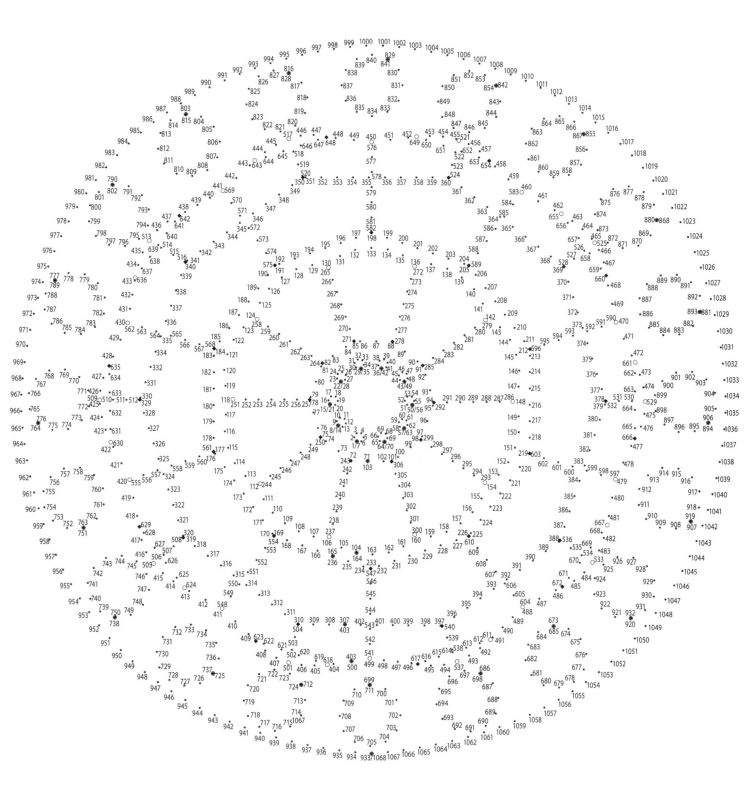

ANSWER KEY

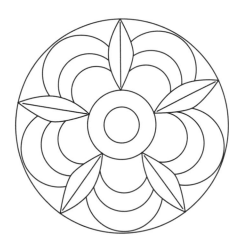

1

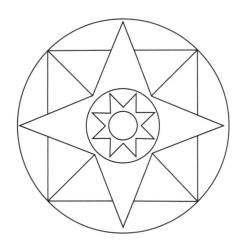

2

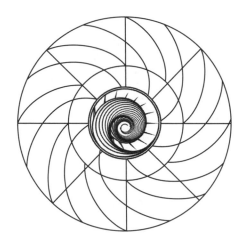

3

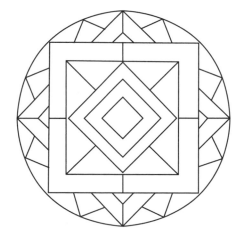

4

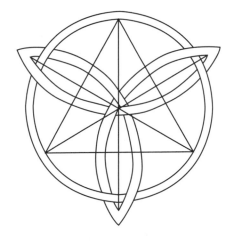

5

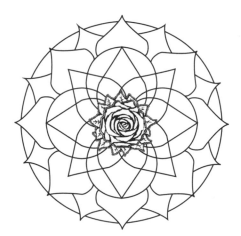

6

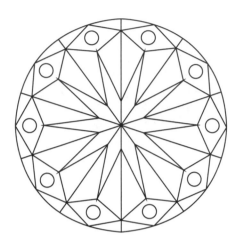

7

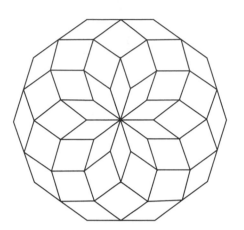

8

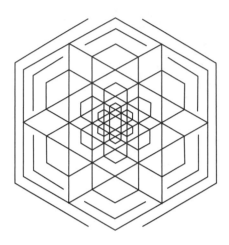

9

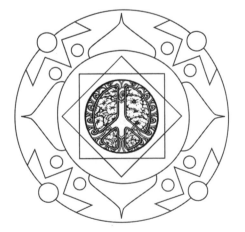

10

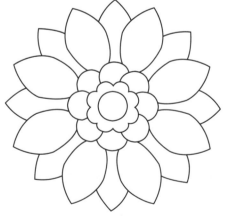

11

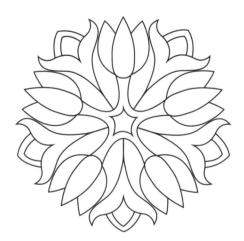

12

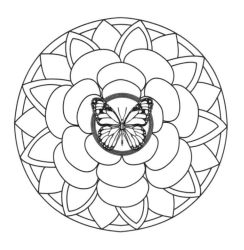

13

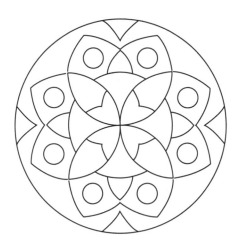

14

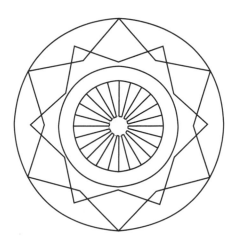

15

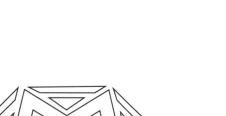

16

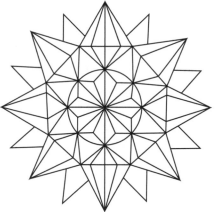

17

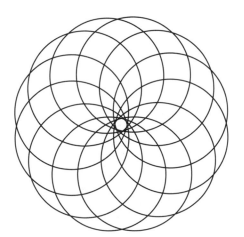

18

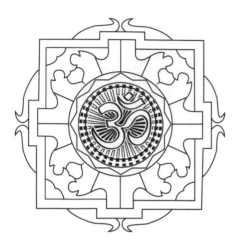

19

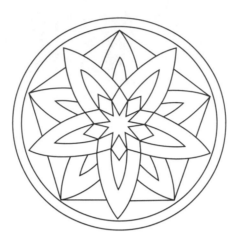

20

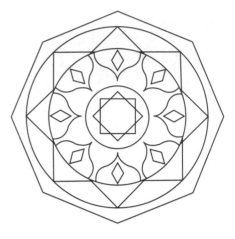

21

22

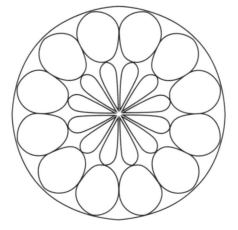

23

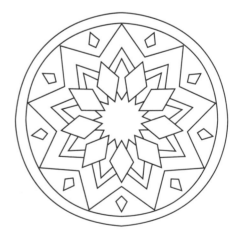

24

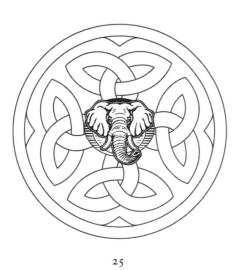

25

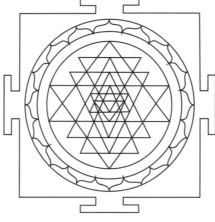

26

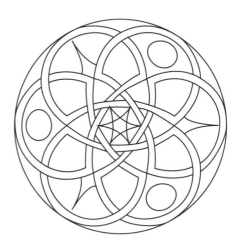

27

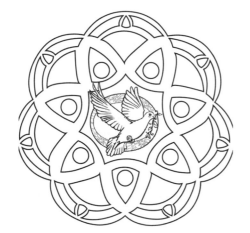

28

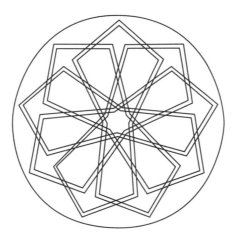

29

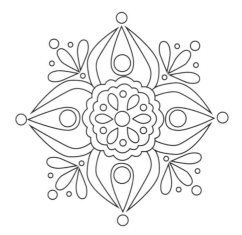

30

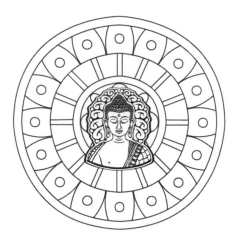

31

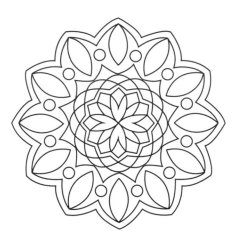

32

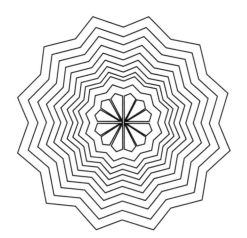

33

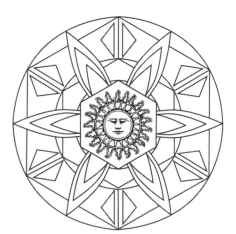

34

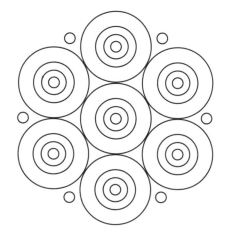

35

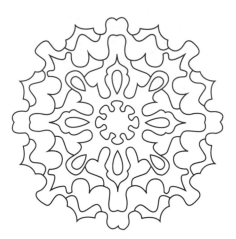

36

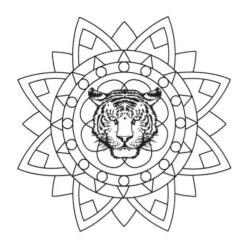

37

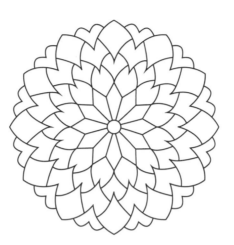

38

39

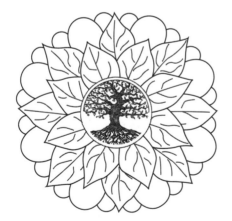

40

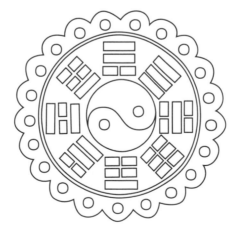

41

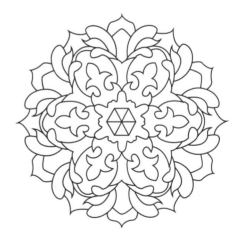

42

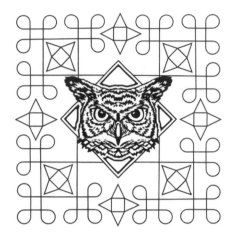

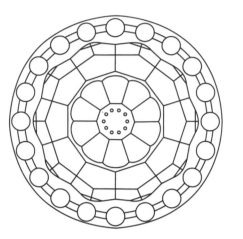

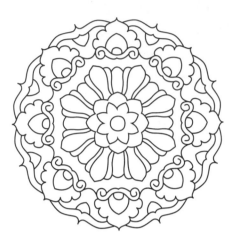

43   44   45